HAL•LEONARD
INSTRUMENTAL PLAY-ALONG

AUDIO
ACCESS
INCLUDED

PLAYBACK+
Speed • Pitch • Balance • Loop

CLARINET

Christmas Carols

T0057411

To access audio visit:
www.halleonard.com/mylibrary
Enter Code
2461-5342-3235-7213

ISBN 978-1-4234-1354-7

Visit Hal Leonard Online at
www.halleonard.com

Contact us:
Hal Leonard
7777 West Bluemound Road
Milwaukee, WI 53213
Email: info@halleonard.com

In Europe, contact:
Hal Leonard Europe Limited
42 Wigmore Street
Marylebone, London, W1U 2RN
Email: info@halleonardeurope.com

In Australia, contact:
Hal Leonard Australia Pty. Ltd.
4 Lentara Court
Cheltenham, Victoria, 3192 Australia
Email: info@halleonard.com.au

CHRIST WAS BORN ON CHRISTMAS DAY

CLARINET

Traditional

DECK THE HALL

CLARINET

Traditional Welsh Carol

THE FIRST NOEL

CLARINET

17th Century English Carol
Music from W. Sandys' *Christmas Carols*

GOOD CHRISTIAN MEN, REJOICE

CLARINET

14th Century Latin Text
14th Century German Melody

GOOD KING WENCESLAS

Words by JOHN M. NEALE
Music from *Piae Cantiones*

CLARINET

With spirit

HARK! THE HERALD ANGELS SING

CLARINET

Words by CHARLES WESLEY
Music by FELIX MENDELSSOHN-BARTHOLDY

I HEARD THE BELLS ON CHRISTMAS DAY

CLARINET

Words by HENRY WADSWORTH LONGFELLOW
Music by JOHN BAPTISTE CALKIN

IT CAME UPON THE MIDNIGHT CLEAR

CLARINET

Words by EDMUND HAMILTON SEARS
Music by RICHARD STORRS WILLIS

JOY TO THE WORLD

CLARINET

Words by ISAAC WATTS
Music by GEORGE FRIDERIC HANDEL

O CHRISTMAS TREE

CLARINET

Traditional German Carol

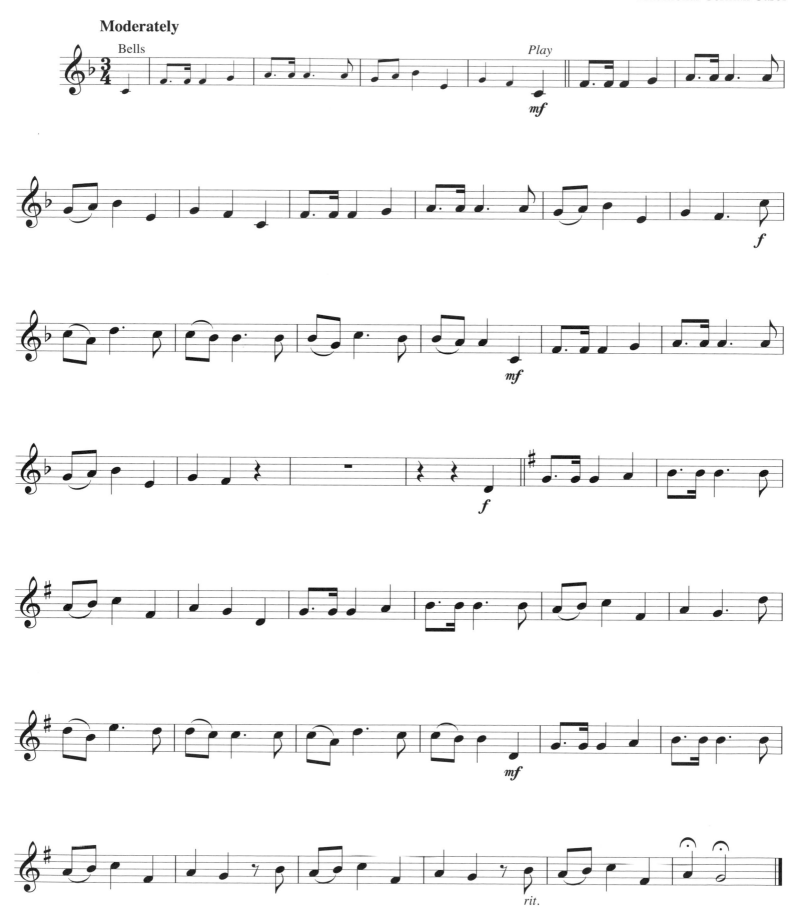

O COME, O COME, EMMANUEL

CLARINET

Plainsong, 13th Century

SING WE NOW OF CHRISTMAS

CLARINET

Traditional

Joyfully

WE THREE KINGS OF ORIENT ARE

CLARINET

Words and Music by
JOHN H. HOPKINS, JR.

WE WISH YOU A MERRY CHRISTMAS

CLARINET

Traditional English Folksong

O LITTLE TOWN OF BETHLEHEM

CLARINET

Words by PHILLIPS BROOKS
Music by LEWIS H. REDNER

Slowly, with feeling

Your favorite songs are arranged just for solo instrumentalists with this outstanding series. Each book includes great full-accompaniment play-along audio so you can sound just like a pro! Check out **www.halleonard.com** to see all the titles available.

The Beatles

All You Need Is Love • Blackbird • Day Tripper • Eleanor Rigby • Get Back • Here, There and Everywhere • Hey Jude • I Will • Let It Be • Lucy in the Sky with Diamonds • Ob-La-Di, Ob-La-Da • Penny Lane • Something • Ticket to Ride • Yesterday.

_____ 00225330	Flute	$14.99
_____ 00225331	Clarinet	$14.99
_____ 00225332	Alto Sax	$14.99
_____ 00225333	Tenor Sax	$14.99
_____ 00225334	Trumpet	$14.99
_____ 00225335	Horn	$14.99
_____ 00225336	Trombone	$14.99
_____ 00225337	Violin	$14.99
_____ 00225338	Viola	$14.99
_____ 00225339	Cello	$14.99

Chart Hits

All About That Bass • All of Me • Happy • Radioactive • Roar • Say Something • Shake It Off • A Sky Full of Stars • Someone like You • Stay with Me • Thinking Out Loud • Uptown Funk.

_____ 00146207	Flute	$12.99
_____ 00146208	Clarinet	$12.99
_____ 00146209	Alto Sax	$12.99
_____ 00146210	Tenor Sax	$12.99
_____ 00146211	Trumpet	$12.99
_____ 00146212	Horn	$12.99
_____ 00146213	Trombone	$12.99
_____ 00146214	Violin	$12.99
_____ 00146215	Viola	$12.99
_____ 00146216	Cello	$12.99

Disney Greats

Arabian Nights • Hawaiian Roller Coaster Ride • It's a Small World • Look Through My Eyes • Yo Ho (A Pirate's Life for Me) • and more.

_____ 00841934	Flute	$12.99
_____ 00841935	Clarinet	$12.99
_____ 00841936	Alto Sax	$12.99
_____ 00841937	Tenor Sax	$12.95
_____ 00841938	Trumpet	$12.99
_____ 00841939	Horn	$12.99
_____ 00841940	Trombone	$12.99
_____ 00841941	Violin	$12.99
_____ 00841942	Viola	$12.99
_____ 00841943	Cello	$12.99
_____ 00842078	Oboe	$12.99

The Greatest Showman

Come Alive • From Now On • The Greatest Show • A Million Dreams • Never Enough • The Other Side • Rewrite the Stars • This Is Me • Tightrope.

_____ 00277389	Flute	$14.99
_____ 00277390	Clarinet	$14.99
_____ 00277391	Alto Sax	$14.99
_____ 00277392	Tenor Sax	$14.99
_____ 00277393	Trumpet	$14.99
_____ 00277394	Horn	$14.99
_____ 00277395	Trombone	$14.99
_____ 00277396	Violin	$14.99
_____ 00277397	Viola	$14.99
_____ 00277398	Cello	$14.99

Movie and TV Music

The Avengers • Doctor Who XI • Downton Abbey • Game of Thrones • Guardians of the Galaxy • Hawaii Five-O • Married Life • Rey's Theme (from *Star Wars: The Force Awakens*) • The X-Files • and more.

_____ 00261807	Flute	$12.99
_____ 00261808	Clarinet	$12.99
_____ 00261809	Alto Sax	$12.99
_____ 00261810	Tenor Sax	$12.99
_____ 00261811	Trumpet	$12.99
_____ 00261812	Horn	$12.99
_____ 00261813	Trombone	$12.99
_____ 00261814	Violin	$12.99
_____ 00261815	Viola	$12.99
_____ 00261816	Cello	$12.99

12 Pop Hits

Believer • Can't Stop the Feeling • Despacito • It Ain't Me • Look What You Made Me Do • Million Reasons • Perfect • Send My Love (To Your New Lover) • Shape of You • Slow Hands • Too Good at Goodbyes • What About Us.

_____ 00261790	Flute	$12.99
_____ 00261791	Clarinet	$12.99
_____ 00261792	Alto Sax	$12.99
_____ 00261793	Tenor Sax	$12.99
_____ 00261794	Trumpet	$12.99
_____ 00261795	Horn	$12.99
_____ 00261796	Trombone	$12.99
_____ 00261797	Violin	$12.99
_____ 00261798	Viola	$12.99
_____ 00261799	Cello	$12.99

Songs from Frozen, Tangled and Enchanted

Do You Want to Build a Snowman? • For the First Time in Forever • Happy Working Song • I See the Light • In Summer • Let It Go • Mother Knows Best • That's How You Know • True Love's First Kiss • When Will My Life Begin • and more.

_____ 00126921	Flute	$14.99
_____ 00126922	Clarinet	$14.99
_____ 00126923	Alto Sax	$14.99
_____ 00126924	Tenor Sax	$14.99
_____ 00126925	Trumpet	$14.99
_____ 00126926	Horn	$14.99
_____ 00126927	Trombone	$14.99
_____ 00126928	Violin	$14.99
_____ 00126929	Viola	$14.99
_____ 00126930	Cello	$14.99

Top Hits

Adventure of a Lifetime • Budapest • Die a Happy Man • Ex's & Oh's • Fight Song • Hello • Let It Go • Love Yourself • One Call Away • Pillowtalk • Stitches • Writing's on the Wall.

_____ 00171073	Flute	$12.99
_____ 00171074	Clarinet	$12.99
_____ 00171075	Alto Sax	$12.99
_____ 00171106	Tenor Sax	$12.99
_____ 00171107	Trumpet	$12.99
_____ 00171108	Horn	$12.99
_____ 00171109	Trombone	$12.99
_____ 00171110	Violin	$12.99
_____ 00171111	Viola	$12.99
_____ 00171112	Cello	$12.99

Wicked

As Long As You're Mine • Dancing Through Life • Defying Gravity • For Good • I'm Not That Girl • Popular • The Wizard and I • and more.

_____ 00842236	Flute	$12.99
_____ 00842237	Clarinet	$12.99
_____ 00842238	Alto Saxophone	$12.99
_____ 00842239	Tenor Saxophone	$11.95
_____ 00842240	Trumpet	$12.99
_____ 00842241	Horn	$12.99
_____ 00842242	Trombone	$12.99
_____ 00842243	Violin	$12.99
_____ 00842244	Viola	$12.99
_____ 00842245	Cello	$12.99